Duh-2000

The Stupidest Things Said About The Year 2000 Problem

By Dave Higgins and Ken Orr

First Printing: February 1999

Introduction

July 2, 1998: The dawn of a new Duh!

Here at the Ken Orr Institute we describe ourselves as a "think thimble" (it's like a "think tank" only smaller and the pay isn't as good). So as you can imagine, good ideas around here are as common as cow pies in a crowded pasture—at least we think that's what people are trying to say when they talk about our ideas. Last summer, we were getting tired of reading all the dis-information, mis-information, and otherwise silly things being said about the Year 2000 problem. Suddenly it struck us like a wet marmot: Let's feature stupid quotes on the web and give away a prize for the stupidest one we find! We had no idea what a deep well we had stumbled into.

Stupidity surrounding Y2k comes in many forms. We have people on one end of the stupid scale in total denial, saying that the Y2k bug isn't a problem and we shouldn't be worrying about it at all. And we have people on the opposite end saying that we should all run for the hills and prepare for "the end of the world as we know it" (or TEOTWAWKI to it's close personal friends*). As consultants, we've made our living trying to teach people and get them to work smarter. We find it ironic in the extreme that stupidity seems to be working out so much better for us. We've discovered a paradox: both knowledge and stupidity are limitless, but somehow there seems to be much more of the latter.

Natually, everyone wants to know what *we* think will happen when the clock rolls over on 1/1/2000. Well, for a small fee we'll be glad to tell you (we are consultants, after all). Here's a hint: we don't particularly advise you to purchase a lot of freeze-dried food or an Ozark hideaway, unless of course you like bad food and sharing it with friends with few teeth.

And where will we be when the clock rolls over? Nowhere near a phone, that's for sure.

-Dave Higgins & Ken Orr, January 1999

*Actually, we try not to make too much fun of the Y2k survivalist types: they have guns and we're pretty easy to find.

A Word About URL's

We're assuming that you, the reader, have spent many a fine hour surfing the net and are well aware that the URL's printed in this book are likely to change without notice or vanish into thin cyberspace. We tried to make sure that all the web pages quoted were current at the time the book was printed, but you know how that goes. Check our website: www.duh-2000.com periodically for the latest in Year 2000 stupidity, and feel free to continue to send us the best stupid statements about the Year 2000 problem at contest@duh-2000.com.

If, however, you've received this book as a present from an internet-savvy friend (or employee or co-worker), then don't sweat the funny-looking words and characters on this page. Just ask them for help...like you usually do.

Oh, and don't write us if you find a typo or two in the quotes and in the titles of the articles quoted: they are reproduced exactly as we found them on the web—typos, grammatical errors, funny spelling and all.

Chapter One:

General Paranoia

We've all heard it many, many times: the Year 2000 problem is all the fault of the programmers. Blaming programmers for the problem is like blaming soldiers for deaths during wartime: yes, they were the ones that pulled the trigger, but their bosses were the ones that told them to. Programmers have known forever that their code had problems—they just didn't know software would last so long. If you want someone to blame, blame the management that put off trying to fix the problem until the last minute. Or, blame someone else, as these people have...

Nicholas Zvegintzov, author and industry pundit: "The Year 2000 problem (years stored by their last two digits will overflow from "99" to "00" when the year passes from 1999 to 2000, causing miscalculations and misunderstandings) is not a huge problem of computer software, nor a unique problem, nor a difficult problem to solve, but it is the focus of a huge and unique racket."

Yet another entry in the "it's all a consultant conspiracy" theory. Quoted on **Software Management Network** "The Year 2000 as Racket and Ruse" (Originally published in **American Programmer**, February 1996). Submitted by Shane Taylor.

http://www.softwaremanagement.com/References/year_2000.html

Gregor Bailar, Executive vice president and chief information officer for the National Association of Securities Dealers on whether your brokerage accounts might get deleted due to Y2k problems: "Ludicrous. But I'll have paper printouts of my personal finances. Just in case."

Don't worry, be happy...and keep your receipts. Quoted on **Forbes** "The Glitch Watch" January 11, 1999. Submitted by Tom Carr.

http://www.forbes.com/forbes/99/0111/6301052a.htm

"Then, a self-described "rainbow gypsy" named **Jason Gibson** grabbed the mike. His face dusted with glitter and framed by a floppy purple velvet cap, Gibson shared Y2K advice he had learned from Hopi elders, urging those in attendance to form "crystal earth pods" and head to the hills. He invited people to join him at a Planet Art Network meeting, where they could get their galactic signature decoded and learn the real cause of Y2K."

The "funny" mushroom crop in Portland must have been very, very good this year. Quoted on **Willamette Week** "Y2k Hippies: Just because they're paranoid doesn't mean they're wrong" December 2, 1998. Submitted by John Shier.
http://www.wweek.com/html/leada120298.html

Tom Beasley, co-operator of Conniry's Native Skills and Wilderness School in the hills just northeast of San Diego: "If this Y2K thing goes all the way it could go to the Stone Age. I don't anticipate that happening, but you never know."

Stone age? I guess once the computers all fail we will forget how to build fires and smelt iron. A must-read article just full of silliness. Quoted on **The Boston Globe** "Gathering gear for 2000" December 8, 1998. Submitted by Stacy Morris.
http://www.boston.com/dailyglobe2/342/nation/Gathering_gear_for_2000+.shtml

An unnamed director for a leading French bank: "The Year 2000 question is a conspiracy cooked up by the Americans and the British to create a smokescreen and distract attention away from preparations for the single European currency."

The surest sign of a vast conspiracy is the utter lack of evidence for one. Pretty darn clever of all those COBOL programmers to have anticipated the Euro back in the 1960's and kept it secret all these years. Quoted on **The Economist** "Countries that count" September 1998. Submitted by L. Clark O'Hare.

http://www.economist.com/editorial/freeforall/19-9-98/bug6.html

An un-named guest speaker at a Dallas area Y2k preparedness forum: "Depending on your view of the situation, the fuel you have at the time of the collapse might be all you have for five years," he says, adding that whatever you do, you shouldn't buy a propane tank. "Rent it," he says. "Pay a $250, two-year down payment, and in two years they're bankrupt. And give 'em your Visa number."

And hope the propane dealer's credit card verification system takes it, of course. We haven't gone after the inherent stupidity in some of the Y2k survivalist literature to date, but this article made for interesting and occasionally humorous reading. Quoted on **The Dallas Observer.com** "Bugged By The Millennium" August 27, 1998.

http://www.dallasobserver.com/1998/082798/ - feature11.html

Hank Erwin of WDJC Radio in Birmingham, Alabama: "I have specifically asked Mr. Hyatt (Michael Hyatt, author of *The Millennium Bug*) to address the Y2K breakdown as it applies to churches. ... Most Alabama churches are still in the dark as to what Y2K is all about. Unless they wake up soon, it could be a disaster!" Of Biblical proportions? Now, if the Telcos and the public utilities, break down, sure...disaster. But *churches*??? Quoted on **MSNBC** "First Y2K briefing set as wake-up call to Alabama churches" August 25, 1998. http://www.msnbc.com/local/WOWL/18841.asp

Chapter Two:

General Stupidity

When we first started the Duh-2000 contest, we argued briefly about whether to call it a contest about being "dumb" or being "stupid." We decided that being dumb is simple and not really worthy of mention—we all do dumb things every day. Being stupid, however, seems to require more effort and is more worthy of notice. Thus, "stupid" won out.

The two most common elements in the universe are hydrogen and stupidity...

Columnist **Enoch Muhammad**: "What caused the designers of computers and computer chip machinery to ignore this mess and who should be blamed? Why is this problem called a bug or a virus? Was this problem planned by the designers or by some hackers?"
It's all a plot. All those smart COBOL programmers were planning their revenge even back then. Or, we could blame short-sighted management for waiting until the last minute before fixing the problem. Nah! Quoted on **The Daily Egyptian** "Shock 19" November 17, 1998. Submitted anonymously.
http://www.dailyegyptian.com/fall98/11-17-98/shock19.html

An unidentified reader of Jake Kirchner's column in PC Magazine: "I really hate it," my correspondent wrote, "when supposedly educated people like yourself don't understand that the new millennium doesn't start until 1/1/2001."
Oh. So if I'm a "millennium purist" I guess I won't have a problem on 1/1/2000. Quoted on **PC Magazine Online** "Bugged by the Year 2000" November 20, 1998. Submitted by Jake Kirchner (we presume).
http://www.zdnet.com/products/stories/reviews/0,4161,247539,00.html

Mark Sainsbury, President of the New Zealand Inbound Tour Operators Committee: " 'When you are talking about respectable airlines like Air New Zealand, you just take it for granted that they will have that covered. They are not going to let their aeroplanes drop out of the sky because of the millennium bug.'
Mr Sainsbury admits ITOC has not yet talked with Air New Zealand about the implications of Y2K. "

But we're sure they are working hard on the problem. Really sure. Really, really sure. No need to worry. Nothing can go wrong. Quoted on **NZInfotechWeekly** "Y2K hasn't scared away tourists booking NZ trips" October 27, 1998.
http://www.infotech.co.nz/october_26/nxtour.html

Giorgio Leskovic, European banking services director for IDC, commenting on why the preparation for the Euro is more important: "In less than four months they have to be ready for monetary union, whereas with year 2000 you have another year."

And if you're behind schedule a little at the end of the year, just have the EU declare an extra one-day bank holiday on Monday, January 3, 2000 so everyone can finish up. Quoted on **Computer Weekly News** "Euro compliance stays top priority" September 10, 1998 (requires free registration).
http://www.computerweekly.co.uk/cwarchive/news/19980910/cwcontainer.asp?name=C7.html

Stupid E-Mail Entrepreneurs

"From: bob [snip] <**subgnbob**@[snip]>

To: Nick@y2kclassifieds.com

Date: Friday, October 23, 1998 4:12 PM Subject: guns?????!!!!!

Im not personally going for the y2k problem being computer litterate. But i would like to sell guns to the people as long as they don't want to bring them back after 2000. Glocks are back ordered from the police purchases so the used ones are all gone. I can get you new ones for $450.00 and Mac90's are around $375.00. I'm sure you can get these prices up there at good guys or one of the other discount shops but thanks for trying me. Your going to have a hard time finding someone who uses a computer who thinks the date is important to the operation but good luck anyway. Bob [snip]"

Will those Mac90's run the new iMac OS? And are those glocks Y2k gompliant??

Thanks to Nick Van Houte at **Y2k Classifieds** for sharing his e-mail with us.

The **Rev. Richard Mooney**, pastor of Church of the Holy Family in Virginia Beach, apparently commenting on Pat Robertson's advice to stock up on supplies for Y2k: "Americans are nuts about religion, and we tend to go particularly nuts about religion in any year that ends in a double zero, and this year has three zeros, so it's even worse. ... I find this Year 2000 nonsense perfectly predictable and utterly non-interesting. ... My advice to those who are worried about the Year 2000 problem is to buy new computers."

We're sure his heart's in the right place, but his technical advice leaves something to be desired. Quoted on **PilotOnline News** "Robertson says stock up to prepare for Year 2000" October 16, 1998. Submitted by Heather Westerfield.
http://www.pilotonline.com/news/nw1016pat.html

Thomas Oleson, research director at IDC: "Ed Yardeni warns of an 80 per cent chance of recession and yet when you look at the fact that Y2K will require only 3.4 per cent of total IT spending in the five years up to the Millennium, we have a good reason for asking him, 'where are you coming from?'"

An informed position, perhaps? Could it be because people are *only* spending 3.4 percent of their IT budgets on the fix? Quoted on **VNU Newswire** "IDC European Forum: Y2k not global catastrophe" September 8, 1998. Submitted by Mark A. Walker and Tom Carr (their e-mails arrived at the same time!).
http://webserv.vnunet.com/www_user/plsql/pkg_vnu_news.right_frame?p_story=62774

James O. Spellman, a spokesman for the Securities Industry Association on the recent pre-test of securities trading Y2k compliance "What we honestly learned was that the year 2000 problem was really small." The article he is quoted in goes on to point out that "The securities industry will spend between $5 billion and $6 billion through 1999 to fix the bug."

A billion here and a billion there and pretty soon you're talking about "small."

Quoted on **ABCNews.com** "Wall Street Tests Y2K" August 10, 1998. Submitted by Fred Holborn.

http://www.abcnews.com/sections/business/DailyNews/y2kbug980810/index.html

Oracle Corporation: "In 60 Days Oracle Can Solve a Problem That Took 2000 Years to Create"

Catchy, yet stupid. Banner headline on their corporate website. Submitted by Andy Maher.

http://www.oracle.com/year2000/

Check it yourself—Advice on how to test your PC for Y2k compliance found in a Florida Telco Credit Union newsletter: "Set the date on your PC to 29 February 2000. Do you get a message, 'invalid date'? You should, as it is a leap year!"

Wait...it gets even better. Our submitter, Diane Wunderlich, called the newsletter's editor's staff to point out the mistake. She was politely told that it was not a mistake, saying "that's right, it is a leap year". Printed in **The Courier: A Publication of Florida Telco Credit Union** "Your Home Computer — Will it Work in the New Millennium" Summer 1998. No URL on this one, but we do have a copy of the publication on file.

"The Gartner Group, which said last year that millennium bomb rehabilitation would cost between $300 billion and $600 billion worldwide, also said in the report published this month that *only 50 percent of companies that had projects to eliminate the bomb planned to test their corrected systems.*"

What? Test? I'm sure it'll work fine. Besides, eliminating that 40-50% of our project timeline gives us a chance to tell our executives we'll be done in time. From **Rueters** "Millennium Computer Bomb Seen Unstoppable For Some" August 19, 1998. By the way for the DUH impaired, it isn't the Gartner Group we're talking about being stupid here.

http://dailynews.yahoo.com/headlines/tc/story.html?s=v/nm/19980819/tc/2000_10.html

David Race Bannon, an instructor in computer sciences at Guilford Technical Community College (Greensboro NC): "If computers turned off tomorrow, who cares? It'd take about a week (to fix). But the computers are not going to turn off. ... The average consumer is not going to have any problem at all. Your microwave will keep on running no matter what date it's set for."

Apparently people are worried about their small appliances. Quoted on **Greensboro News & Record Online** "Y2K doomsday: fact or fiction?" August 2, 1998. Submitted by Mark Doerhoefer.

http://www.greensboro.com/nronline/business/y2k02.htm

Nicholas Zvegintzov, president and chief technical officer of Software Management Network: "...much computer software interprets two-digit years perfectly well. (If you are not confused because your driver's license expires in 01, why should a computer be confused?)"

Only the software that uses the two-digit year to do any kind of calculation will be confused. Quoted on **IntellectualCapital.com** "Don't Move to that Y2K Commune Just Yet" June 25, 1998. Submitted by Jeanne M. Viola.

http://www.intellectualcapital.com/issues/98/0625/iccon.asp

Judy Noe, technology consultant: "It's not Armageddon. The sun won't fall out of the sky because it's not controlled by computers."
Good thing. There would have to be one honking big heat sink on that particular embedded chip. Quoted in the **Chicago Tribune** "Bunker mentality taking hold in fear of Y2k glitch" August 3, 1998. Submitted by Jim Ritchhart.
http://chicagotribune.com/business/businessnews/ws/item/0,1267,9693-9678-12724,00.html

Ric Edelman, author, radio investment advisor, and faculty member at Georgetown University: "Be aware of the Millennium Bug, but don't do anything about it."
Finally! Some advice that senior executives, politicians and bureaucrats will have no problem understanding. Quoted on the **Metro DC Fairfax Journal** "Are your investments safe from the Bug?" August 11, 1998. Submitted by Paul Milne.
http://www.jrnl.com/news/98/Aug/jrn29110898.html

Not a quote, but a special Duh-2000 tip of the hat to:
Merrill Lynch, (nominated elsewhere for painting a rosy picture of corporate Y2k readiness) who just disclosed in their recent SEC-10k filing that their Y2k remediation effort would be $100 million (US) more costly than the $275 million (US) they said it would in March 1998.

Oopsie! This from the company that just released a report saying that most businesses were in good shape. Read about their report in the **TechWeb** article "Merrill Lynch Paints Rosy Y2K Picture" July 10, 1998, and about their new estimate on the **VNU Newswire** "Merrill Lynch forced to add $100 million to Y2K costs" August 11, 1998.

http://www.techweb.com/wire/story/y2k/TWB19980710S0002

http://webserv.vnunet.com/www_user/plsql/pkg_vnu_news.right_frame?p_story=60866

James Annable, chief economist at First Chicago NBD: "Will there be glitches? Absolutely. Will it cause a recession? Absolutely not. Will it cause the end of the world? The question should be, 'What are you smoking?'"

AND

Steve Roach, chief economist at Morgan Stanley Dean Witter: "There is not one shred of evidence that suggests that year-2000 compliance or non-compliance will have any effect on the U.S. business cycle."

A "two for one" article from **Fox News** "Economists Debate Global Impact of Year 2000" July 1, 1998.

http://www.foxnews.com/js_index.sml?content=/scitech/070198/y2kecon.sml

Pat Buchanan and Bill Press, Co-hosts of CNN's Crossfire: "Let me tell you something. I have been doing the show two and a half years, every day we have started on time. When you got a deadline, it seems to me, you get there." and "I'm a total skeptic on this, I think this whole thing is a total fraud. You can't tell me they're not going to fix it."

Ok, we won't. Spoken like a true executive who has never managed a real project, during "Year 2000: Will the World's Computers Crash?" **CNN's Crossfire** Interview with Peter de Jager, aired July 14, 1998. Attributed to Pat Buchanan on the transcript but apparently said by Bill Press.

Stupid Y2k Notices

Received by an insurance policy holder in the UK: "Sir, I have received notice of my house buildings insurance renewal. An enclosure lists various exclusions, among which is 'loss or damage caused by equipment failing correctly to recognise data representing year 2000'. The accompanying policy schedule shows the insurance period to be January 1, 1999, to January 1, 1900."

Oopsie. Found on **The London Times** Letters to the Editor, December 11, 1998. Submitted by Paul Peterson.

http://www.sunday-times.co.uk/news/pages/tim/98/12/11/timopnolt01001.html?1733620

Chapter Three:

Stupid Journalism

The mass media has really outdone themselves on the Y2k issue. First of all, *in every single article* they feel compelled to explain what the Y2k problem is (like there is someone on the planet that hasn't heard of it yet). And, to read most reports, you would gather that the biggest problem areas are 1) planes falling from the sky, 2) elevators, and 3) small kitchen appliances, especially microwave ovens and sometimes toasters.

The other thing you quickly learn is that most journalists could really use some better editing...

Columnist **Anita Creamer**: "If the threat is so great, why is the name so cute? Y2K sounds like a baby's first sentence or the name of a stuffed successor to Furby or, at the very least, a quirky, jerky, utterly appealing "Star Wars" character. Y2K sounds as friendly and precious as a puppy."

My nephew got a Furby for Christmas. If the Y2k problem is half as annoying as those things, we're in deep do-do. And, as of this writing, Lucasfilms is absolutely mum on whether "Y2K" is actually a character in the new Star Wars film. Quoted on **The Sacramento Bee** "Y2K: Head for hills or nearest chat room" January 1, 1999. Submitted by Judy Hoskins.

http://www.sacbee.com/voices/sac/creamer/creamer_19990101.html

David Houghton, financial columnist for the Ottawa Sun: "According to one article I read from a highly regarded analyst, the big guys, the banks and so forth, have solved their Y2K problem already or will have it in hand very shortly. The mid-cap guys are still working on in and only the small guy is in left field. That could be a problem, but remember, the small guy can do a lot with a paper, pencil and calculator that the big guy can't."

And don't forget what they can do with a couple of tin cans and some string by the light of kerosene lamps! Quoted on **The Ottawa Sun** "Canuck stocks lag behind U.S." December 28, 1998. Submitted by Heather Westerfield.

http://www.canoe.ca/OttawaBusiness/OS.OS-12-28-0054.html

"It's one minute after midnight on Dec, 1, 1999. With 31 days left until the new century kicks in and the second 1,000 years in recorded history begins, Americans are wary enough to take few dollars out of their bank accounts, just in case."

Er, excuse us, but the whole "2000 vs. 2001" start of the new millennium issue aside, shouldn't that be the start of the *third* thousand years? And—due to popular demand—we should also point out that there were, in fact, one or two things that happened in recorded history before Y1. Quoted on **The Billings Gazette** "Y2K: Truth or SCARE The sky may not fall, but Y2K is one big thunderhead" January 10, 1999. Submitted by Michael Kenniston.

http://www.billingsgazette.com/business/990110_bus001.html

"Problems in Social Security computers would affect older Americans who rely on the checks to help them in their retirement. For example, an eligible recipient born in 1930 would be recognized as born in 1830 without the computer fix, and could be presumed dead and removed from the rolls. "

Reporters who make up stuff like this should be presumed brain-dead and ignored. Quoted on **Reuters** "Social Security Y2K problems solved" December 28, 1998. Submitted by Jeanne Boyd.

http://www.zdnet.com/zdnn/stories/news/0,4586,2179679,00.html

Op/Ed columnist **David Boldt**: "Experience has taught us, for better or worse, that the events we anticipate almost never occur. Remember Comet Kohoutek?"

Yep, we do. And it's not so much the big Y2k bugs we've thought of that will likely cause problems, but all the little ones no one thought of. Quoted on **The Philadelphia Inquirer** "Barring any real tragedy, it might be fun if computer shink it's 1900" January 5, 1999. Submitted by Heather Westerfield.

http://www.phillynews.com/inquirer/99/Jan/05/opinion/BOLD05.htm

"Bennett's Senate Year 2000 Committee has been looking into how the bug will affect important sectors of the economy, particularly transportation, electricity, health care and other vital services such as drinking water. At the state-of-the-art Lenain Water Treatment Plant overlooking this city of 300,000 south of Los Angeles, officials gave the senator a tour and went over precautions they have taken. The steps go well beyond the simple expedient already known to many home computer operators, said Greg Russell, the plant's senior electrical engineer. That solution is to "fool" one's computer by setting the date to December 1983. Since 1984's days of the weeks and months match 2000's, only the year would be wrong."

And the days of the week. Check your calendars folks: although 1984 *was* a leap year, it started on a Sunday, not a Saturday. Hint: try 1972. Quoted on **AP** via **Hot CoCo** "Water groups ready for 2000 glitch" December 19, 1998. Submitted by Kent Hansen.

http://www.hotcoco.com/news/statfront/kbk03664.htm

Gwynneth Flower, head of the UK Government's millennium bug task force Action 2000: "We are talking about people having a judicious amount of surplus food in their kitchen cupboards. Anyone sensible would plan for this."
AND
A spokeswoman for Sainsbury said: "We feel fairly confident that everything will be normal next year. Much of our millennium preparation is going on alcohol because we think people will be drinking more. We are renting an extra 400,000 sq ft of warehouse space for all that surplus booze."
So at least in the UK it's official: if you can't heat the food you've stockpiled due to a lack of power, you will at least be able to get drunk. Quoted on **The Observer** "Millenium bug panic warning" December 13, 1998. Submitted by Laura Archbald.
http://reports.guardian.co.uk/articles/1998/12/13/38148.html

Editorial by **James K. Glassman** fellow at the American Enterprise Institute: "...Something you know about in advance is unlikely to hurt you very much"
Let's see, we know there will be a big earthquake in California at some point in the future, we know there will be hurricanes each fall... Quoted in the **Washington Post** "Going bonkers over Y2K" December 2, 1998. Submitted first by Heather Westerfield, and also submitted by Bill Adsit and Alan Park.
http://www.bergen.com/morenews/glass01199812026.htm

"The January 1, 2000, better known as the Y2K problem, is not only the bug biting the software industry. Software programmes with in-bulit calendar will also blink out when it comes to February 30, 2000. Virtually none of the present-day software programs are programmed to accept February 30 as a valid date."

And with good reason, we might add! Ok, one more time: 2000 IS a leap year, but it's not that much of a leap year! Quoted on **Indian Express Online (Bombay)** "After Y2K, it is February 30 bug biting" December 20, 1998. Submitted by David Miller.

http://www.expressindia.com/newads/intel/19981221/3550249.htm

Commentary by **Charley Reese**: "If my computer ever tells me, "Sorry, old chap, but I can't write 2,000," I'll just say, "Don't sweat it, old chip. Just leave the space blank, and I'll write in the date." ... To save all an e-mail, I already know that I'm computer-illiterate, and I don't care and do not wish to be educated on this topic. If you want to chew your nails about Y2K, be my guest."

So, let's see if we have this right. Something has to be TEOTWAWKI before we attempt to fix it before it breaks? Or take reasonable precautions in case other people don't fix important things? Quoted on **The Orlando Sentinel** "Forecast: Y2K will not be the end of civilization as we know it" December 15, 1998. Submitted first by Stephen Mahan.

http://www.orlandosentinel.com/opinion/121598_REESE15.html

Canadian Broadcasting Corporation (CBC) Commentator **Rex Murphy**: "We are headed, in a matter of mere months, for the information ice age. The machines are going to freeze and everything that they run — which is everything that runs, will freeze with them. There is nothing in the modern world, from cars to airplanes to hair dryers to TV sets; from Internet accounts to video games, nuclear defense systems to voice mail; from your Bay card to little Johnny's academic standing since grade two; from Revenue Canada to the local gas station, that doesn't owe its proper functioning and record to some computer chip. ... Come the year 2000, when we're all sitting in the dark and huddled around a million living room camp fires, writing messages to one another on paper with $50 pencils and using $3,000 laptops to block out the draughts, $80-billion Bill and the other princelings of Silicon Valley should have been made to pay for what their hucksterism and hubris have cost us."

Trust us, you'll want to see this. Pound-for-pound this is the *stupidest* Y2k report we've seen (and as you can imagine, we've seen a lot!) Congratulations, Rex, you got every single fact wrong. Hair dryers??? Quoted on **CBC's The National** "Point Of View: Y2k" November 2, 1998. Or you can watch the stupidity on RealVideo. Submitted by Russell Hauser. An update: Since this appeared on our web site we heard from several Canadian viewers who indicated that Rex is somewhat of a curmudgeon and was just being sarcastic. You be the judge.

The Text: http://www.tv.cbc.ca/national/pgminfo/rex/pov981102.html

The Video: http://www.tv.cbc.ca/national/real_video/rex981102.ram

Columnist **Paul Kedrosky**: "Let's say that there's a 10 percent chance of something going wrong in a company come January 3, 2000 (January 1st is a Saturday — we'll all sleep through any apocalypse). And imagine that probability is the same at other companies with which the company does business. ... The probability of two companies having a problem is the square of 0.1, or 1%. And the probability of enough companies simultaneously having a problem to return us to the Stone Ages is 0.1 to a very large power — effectively zero. But you wouldn't know that from the "experts." Who knows what math they're doing? Likely none at all."

Hmmm...wonder what the chances were of just one transformer coil failing in New England on November 9, 1965? Quoted on the **National Post Online** "The Year 2000 problem is as silly and annoying as Monica Lewinsky" November 17, 1998. Submitted by David Brevner.

http://www.nationalpost.com/financialpost.asp?f=981117/2024660&s2=opinion

James Derk, Computer Research Editor for The Evansville Courier:

> "Before we get on to reader questions, I'd just like to announce I have solved the Year 2000 crisis. Unless you live in a foxhole, you know that the world as we know it will cease to exist at midnight on Dec. 31, 1999. That's because all of the computers and electronic devices in the world will think it's the year 1900 instead of 2000.
>
> My solution?
>
> Agree with the computers.
>
> We have a golden opportunity here, what we used to call a "do-over" on the playground.
>
> We simply agree that it really is 1900 again. We adjust our clocks all the time, why not our calendar?
>
> (Hint: Take your money out of the stock market on Oct. 20, 1929, keep an eye on the Germans in the 1930s and invest heavily in IBM and Microsoft.) "

An electronic mulligan? It might work. And be sure to speak to Captain Grace Hopper in the 1950's so that COBOL is defined with a four digit default year so we don't have this problem again the next time. Quoted on **Evansville Indiana Courier Electronic Edition** "Y2K bug not nearly as difficult as it seems" November 9, 1998. Submitted by Heather Westerfield

http://courier.evansville.net/cgi/view.cgi?/199811/09/+JDerk_business.html+19981109

Technology columnist **Alan Abrams**: "Personally, I'm worried about peanut butter. What if those peanut-harvesting machines go out of whack on Y2K Day and ruin our best peanut fields? What if the machines at the factory that makes that great stuff with the peanut butter and jelly in the same jar start putting in only jelly? What will I do then? What will I put on my crackers? So I'm going out and buying enough peanut butter to last me at least five years because it will probably take that long for the peanut butter market to recover. But will that be enough?

We think Alan has his tongue stuck firmly in his cheek in this article (or perhaps stuck to the roof of his mouth). Quoted on **The Journal of Commerce** "Millennia madness" October 15, 1998. Submitted by Sara Marshall.

http://www.joc.com/issues/981015/e1dit/e10150.htm

Technical advice columnist and self-described Microsoft Defector **Alex St. John**: "Can you think of any other situations where a computer would have to deal correctly with a date that is sometime in the year 2000? Driver's license expiration, passports, canned goods expiration, etc.. Are you aware of any of the services that depend on this breaking down catastrophically? No. That's because it's no big deal. Any given piece of complex software is guaranteed to contain dozens if not hundreds or even thousands of bugs. Y2K is probably almost always the least of them. Systems that had the date limitations are very old, most of societies electronic infrastructure is built on modern systems. Even if they weren't, the problems associated would be cropping under every circumstance that a date exceeding the year 2000 needs to be stored, which is very often even today. If a breakdown is in the works, it started years ago. Y2K is just a great way to sell newspapers to the technologically illiterate. The only problem will be hysteria, don't loose any sleep over it."

Yeah. We're sure no programmer on the planet will be losing any sleep anytime between now and then. Or working any overtime. Or going to any New Year's Eve parties. Quoted on **Boot Magazine** "Y2K Apocalypse" July 17, 1998. Submitted by Alex Robinson.

http://www.bootnet.com/askalex/987171856.html

Rob Morse, technology columnist: "Y2K is practically a cult already. "Repent, the end is near" has been replaced by "Reboot, 2000 is near." .. Why is it I'm not scared? Is it because I have an iMac that's Y2K compliant? Yes, downloading dominatrixes, an obedient little computer is called "compliant." "

An interesting attitude given that the only two things that an iMac can plug into are the two biggest things that may fail. Quoted on the **San Francisco Examiner** "Gonna party like it's 1899" October 22, 1998.

http://www.sfgate.com/cgi-bin/article.cgi?file=/examiner/archive/1998/10/22/NEWS5090.dtl

Rob Morse, columnist for the San Francisco Examiner: "You bet. I'm going to call a $250-an-hour consultant to reset my microwave. My microwave doesn't know what year it is, and my toaster isn't run by a mainframe computer."

AND

"To me, the Y2K problem is the why-to-care problem, and not just because I'm semi-prepared for the earth to move and return us to 1906 - the heck with 1900."

More toaster concerns. Actually, it was hard to pick just two stupid statements from this column. Quoted on the **San Francisco Examiner** "The media in bed with millennium bug" August 25, 1998. Submitted first by Charles Cherry, but several other alert readers sent us the article as well. Way to go Rob!

http://www.sfgate.com/cgi-bin/article.cgi?file=/examiner/archive/1998/08/25/NEWS6784.dtl

Andrew Tobias, investment advisor, responding to e-mail received from an earlier article on Y2k and investment strategies...

> "From John Wildenthal: There are a few verified examples of embedded chip failures. You might look at www.cv.nrao.edu/y2k/sighting.htm for some verified problems, including the valve at a UK nuclear plant (scram/failsafe in 20 seconds after Y2K).
>
> Power generation (except for windmills, hydroelectric, and solar) is a process of boiling water-spinning turbines-cooling water, over and over. The fan problem you discussed is evidently not uncommon in automated water valves. DeJager's Damocles site mentioned that in the context of a sewer plant until DeJager shut Damocles down.

A.T.: I'm not entirely certain what this means or who DeJager is. Damocles I knew in a previous life. (High school, that is.) "

Dispensing Y2k investment advice, yet apparently unaware of what an embedded chip problem means or who Peter de Jager is... Quoted on **Ameritrade** "Y2K Feedback" August 26, 1998.

http://www.ameritrade.com/cgi-bin/tobias_article.cgi/19980826.html

Lloyd Grove Washington Post Staff Writer: "And let's not omit the looming horror of the "Y2K Scenario" — in which the world's myriad computer systems, which control every aspect of modern life, will crash immediately after midnight on Jan. 1, 2000, because of an unbelievably stupid foul-up by software nerds, and thus plunge the planet into an unimaginable technological apocalypse."

Yep. Software nerds caused the problem all by themselves, with almost no help whatsoever from management and executives. Quoted on **The WashingtonPost.com** "Is the Party Over?" September 1, 1998.
http://www.washingtonpost.com/wp-srv/WPlate/1998-09/01/070l-090198-idx.html

Joseph Nocera, reporter for Money magazine: "Ultimately, what the Y2K alarmists discount most is human adaptability. An astonishingly resilient species, we cope with wars, huge upheavals, natural disasters of all sorts. And now we're going to be stopped in our tracks by a computer glitch? I don't think so."

Not at all. I'm sure we'll adapt. We can, for instance, keep warm by burning old Money magazines for heat if things don't get fixed because reporters convince people this isn't a real problem. This is yet another article with lots of stupid quotes to choose from. Quoted in **Money** "Worried About The Year 2000 Problem? Get Real" September, 1998. Submitted by Dave Howard.
http://web.lexis-nexis.com/more/cahners/11379/3725729/4

In the almost-but-not-quite-right category:

> The number of personal computers subject to the Year 2000 problem is a matter of guesswork — in part because the flaw has so many manifestations. Among the parts of the personal computer that may be affected are:
>
> * CMOS (Complementary Metal Oxide Semiconductor). A small battery-powered source of instructions for the computer, the CMOS stores date information that could be incorrect come 2000.
>
> * BIOS (Basic Input-Output System). Another set of basic computer instructions that manages the flow of data between the computer's operating system and its hardware. The BIOS is often responsible for correctly interpreting the date information received from the CMOS.

Oh really? We've never heard it explained quite like that before. Don't reporters have anyone working with them that knows anything about PC's? Quoted on **The Detroit News online** "It will take lots of guesswork to find parts affected by 2000 date bug" September 10, 1998. For the acronym-challenged, CMOS is the *type* of chip that the BIOS is stored on and not a separate set of instructions...
http://detnews.com/1998/cyberia/9809/10/09100030.htm

Columnist **Rebecca L. Eisenberg** a.k.a. "Net Skink": "Fortunately, like most computer problems, the Y2K bug can be fixed. In many cases, including the huge databases where it strikes the deepest blows, it already has been fixed by programmers who built patches and re-wrote code. Unfortunately, like most computer problems, the Y2K bug's potential dangers have been exaggerated — in this case, to science fiction proportions that humble the supercomputer HAL in Arthur C. Clarke's sci-fi classic, '2001.'"

"I'm sorry Dave. I'm afraid I can't do that." Quoted on **The San Francisco Examiner online** "Year 2000 hype is relentless" April 19, 1998. Submitted by A. Lizard.

http://www.examiner.com/skink/skinkApr19.html

Fred Moody, author and columnist: "When it comes to the fizzle factor—the degree to which an expected event fails to live up to its hype—the "millennium bug" (aka Y2K) will prove to be the standard against which all other overhype is measured. Not for 1,000 years or so has so much dread been provoked, and so much money made, in preparation for something that will amount to so little."

And of course we all know that the Titanic was "hyped" as unsinkable. Quoted on **ABCNews.com** "It's Y1K All Over Again". Submitted by D. Neufeldt.

http://www.abcnews.com/sections/tech/FredMoody/moody64.html

Unidentified editorial writer: "The truth is that it's all about money. And believe us, there are lots of people making huge bucks off your ill-founded panic — and smiling and laughing all the way to the bank."... "Even a lowly mere testing analyst is pulling in 54,300 clams every 12 months — and you can bet that most of them are about 19 years old, listen to Hole and wear a backwards baseball cap."

Hmm...of course this has nothing at all to do with the laws of supply and demand. And what's wrong with Hole? Quoted on the Wichita Business Journal "Y2K: Big windfall for computer geeks" August 24, 1998.
http://www.amcity.com/wichita/stories/082498/tidbits.html

"Now the august Federal Reserve has joined in the year 2000 nonsense. The Fed is commissioning an extra $50 billion in currency for the year 1999 in case the Y2K bug bites. Sociologically, the Fed is correct; mathematically, it is not, because one of two things will happen: Nothing, in which case the extra cash is not needed, or we revert to the year 1900, in which case the dollar will go a lot further because prices were lower then."

And editorial writers a lot smarter. An anonymous entry found on the **Knoxville News Sentinel** editorial page G2, August 23, 1998. No URL for this one, but we have a copy of the article on file.

Chapter Four:

Cluelessness in Government

Your tax dollars at work. Or not, depending on how you look at it...

Capt. Allan Toole, who was recently assigned to correct the Year 2000 (Y2K) problems at the Defense Special Weapons Agency (DSWA) after that agency claimed that three of five so-called "mission critical" computer systems, essential to conducting its most primary duties, were fully prepared to face the computer crisis despite never conducting necessary testing: "I have a good feeling about Y2K in this agency."

We have a good feeling too. How about a big ol' group hug and we'll just forget about it. Suddenly, the U.S. governments' plan to be compliant by March 1999 becomes a bit clearer. Quoted in **USA Today** "Pentagon exaggerated Y2K readiness" December 27, 1998. Submitted by Fred Holborn.

http://www.usatoday.com/life/cyber/tech/ctd907.htm

"In Lowndes County [Alabama], Administrator **Jacquelyn Thomas** said her office is buying a new computer system this year, which she hopes will eliminate any potential problems. Only some county functions are computerized, she said. ... She said her office isn't testing any existing computer systems or equipment. 'We feel we'll be all right,' she said. "

She must have been talking to Capt. Toole at DSWA. From **AP** and quoted on **Alabama Live** "Officials leery of Y2K problems taking precautions" December 8, 1998. Submitted by Bill Adsit.

http://flash.al.com/cgi-bin/al_nview.pl?/home1/wire/AP/Stream-Parsed/BAMA_NEWS/j1771_PM_AL—Y2KReadiness

Denver Colorado's Y2k director **Dave Bufalo**: "We'll oftentimes just wait until the clock rolls over to see if things work or don't work ... I don't think the world's going to come to an end. But I can't say exactly what will happen, either."

If it ain't broke (yet) don't fix it (yet). Besides, there will be *lots* more time to fix things if we wait until after they break. Quoted on the **Denver Post Online** "City to tackle Y2K when time comes" December 13, 1998.

http://www.denverpost.com/news/news1213a.htm

"A worst-case scenario would still allow MSD's waste-treatment plants to operate, Mr. Nalley told commissioners, because of backup electrical systems and manual operation of plant equipment. ... Moreover, he said many sewer systems work via gravity — with backup electrical generators — and would remain operational despite a computer shutdown."

We hadn't realized gravity needed backup electrical generators. Or had a Y2k problem, for that matter. Hopefully any failures will be very localized. Quoted on **The Cincinnati Enquirer** "Sewers to be safe from Y2k?" December 15, 1998. Submitted by Joel Kneisley. And yes, we know they're talking about the other sewer systems, but the idea of gravity being non-Y2k compliant struck us as humorous, so we included it anyway.

http://enquirer.com/editions/1998/12/15/loc_sewers_to_be_safe.html

"The Kenyan government has formed a committee to investigate problems that may be caused by the so-called millennium bug — but its final report is due to be published months after the much-prophesised collapse of non-compliant computer systems. ... The Daily Nation newspaper reported that the government formed the committee on October 19 and ordered a final report on the consequences of the millennium bug in 18 months time."

Maybe they want the final report to include how effective the disaster recovery plan was. Quoted on **Reuters** "Kenya millennium bug report to finish in April 2000" November 2, 1998. Submitted by Tom Lion.

http://guide-p.infoseek.com/Content?arn=a0462LBY655reulb-19981102&col=NX

"With a self-imposed September 1999 deadline looming, Chinese government agencies and government-owned enterprises are hard at work tackling the millennium bug, the China Economic Times said Wednesday. ... The State Council, or Cabinet, decreed last month that all government computer systems must be revised by March, and millennium bug tests must be completed by September 1999. Those that fail to meet the deadlines will be punished."

The floggings will continue until morale improves. Quoted on **CNET News.com** "China sprays for Y2K bugs" October 21, 1998. Submitted by Tom Lion.

http://www.news.com/News/Item/0,4,27792,00.html?st.ne.ni.rel

Federal Reserve Chairman **Alan Greenspan**, testifying before the Senate in July: "I'm one of the culprits who created this problem...I used to write those programs back in the '60s and '70s and was so proud of the fact that I was able to squeeze a few elements of space out of my program by not having to put 19 before the year."
-AND-
Federal Reserve Chairman **Alan Greenspan** testifying before congress in September: "I have no question that we're going to have very unusual things occurring."
Well, I guess he would know... The first quote is from the **Kansas City Star** "Chances to fix problem squandered for decades" September 26, 1998, and the second is from **USA Today** "Survey: Y2K woes won't sink economy" September 30, 1998. Submitted by Jon Wiley.
http://www.kcstar.com/item/pages/y2k.pat,business/30da66a5.926,.html
http://www.usatoday.com/life/cyber/tech/ctd554.htm

Sally Katzen, Director OMB: "The Year 2000 Problem Will Be A Non-Event For The Federal Government"
What would qualify as an "event?" A meteor the size of Texas? Testimony before the House Subcommitte on Government Management, Information, and Technology on July 10, 1997 and quoted on the **y2kinvestor**, "The Year 2000 Problem Will Devastate The Global Economy"
http://www.y2kinvestor.com/intro.html

Special Section: The Russians and Y2k

Vladislav Petrov, spokesman for the Russia's Atomic Energy Ministry: "We don't have any problems yet. We'll deal with the problem in the year 2000."
This from the people that cheerfully brought you Chernobyl, found in the **AP** article "Experts Fear 2000 Computer Glitch" July 4, 1998
http://dailynews.yahoo.com/headlines/ap/technology/story.html?s=v/ap/980704/technology/stories/bugged_by_millennium_1.html

Marshal **Igor Sergeyev**, former commander of Strategic Missile Forces: "This problem affects more those spheres where mass-market computer technology is used. In Russia's Strategic Missile Forces, there is no risk because special computer technology is used."
Oh. "Special" computers. Why didn't they just say so in the first place? Quoted on **Wired News** "Russia Brushes Off Y2K Scare" August 12, 1998. Submitted by Mavis Thomson-Shearer.
http://www.wired.com/news/news/politics/story/14380.html

Andrei Terekov, a St. Petersburg University mathematics professor and director of Lanit Holding—a firm helping Russian companies with the Y2k transition—on the likelihood that the Y2K problem would cause Russian warheads to detonate or missiles to be fired by mistake: "My understanding is that the problem with strategic weapons has been solved."

Problem? There was a problem!? We thought they were using "special" computers (see Contest #3) that didn't *have* problems. Quoted on **USA Today** "Expert downplays Y2k nuclear effect" January 14, 1999.
http://www.usatoday.com/life/cyber/tech/cte159.htm

A spokesman for the Russian Defense Ministry: "There is a problem and we are working on it."

Buzz...snap...crackle...er...Houston, we have a problem. We guess their "special" computers weren't so special after all. Quoted on **Russia Today/Reuters Russian** "Military Says Y2k Bug A Problem, U.S. Helps" January 26, 1999.
http://www.russiatoday.com/rtoday/news/99012607.html

Mikhail Salnikov, chief editor of Compulog magazine: "The first problem for us was that we believed up until a year ago that the 2000 problem was not a serious threat. ... Unfortunately, many specialists left the state sector and went to the commercial market during perestroika (under former Soviet leader Mikhail Gorbachev in the 1980s) and now there are not many people left in the public sector to assess this problem. ... Russia can solve this problem herself."

Uh huh. Apparently they have "special" programmers as well as "special" computers. Quoted on **Reuters** "Russia Sees Transport Problems From Millennium Bug" January 28, 1999. Submitted by Linda Fitzpatrick.

http://dailynews.yahoo.com/headlines/tc/story.html?s=v/nm/19990128/tc/russiay2k_5.html

An Unnamed editor-in-chief of a Russian computer newspaper: "I don't see any disaster. The great Russian god "Luck" will help us. We are not a country as computerized as America. In *their* country there are terminals rejecting credit cards expiring after 2000. In *their* country the burning of a big business-center ruined thousand of companies that had their offices there, because their computers burned. We do not fear it, because here, out of absurdity, all is recorded on paper in parallel, and accountancy is recorded on paper. Should all collapse, companies will invite intelligent students who, for little money, will repair all in one month. Our disaster will be hundred times less than in America. As for our army... nothing will happen. It is already in a shape that cannot be worse."

We thought all the intelligent Russian students were already working for US Y2k contracting firms. Even more reassuring news from the country formerly known as the Soviet Union. Quoted on the Russian Y2k site http://www.year2000.ru/Press/Ogonyok-0298.html (warning: the site is in Russian...so make sure you have your Cyrillic font installed). Submitted and translated from the Russian by Thierry Falissard.

Special Section: John Koskinen, US Y2k Czar

John Koskinen: "Would we do better if I stood up tomorrow and said this is a national crisis?"

Uh, yep. Quoted in **Time** "Why The Government's Machines Won't Make It" June 15, 1998.
http://www.pathfinder.com/time/magazine/1998/dom/980615/technology_why_the_gover.html

John Koskinen when asked how the Federal Emergency Management Agency (FEMA) was preparing for Y2K: "Well, we've been trying to get them to focus on this problem."

Try harder, John. If only one agency of the Federal government is to have a plan for Y2k, one would think it should be FEMA, wouldn't one? Quoted on **Westergaard Year 2000** "Federal Government is Botching Year 2000 Efforts" by Jim Lord (who knows what he's talking about) September 21, 1998.
http://y2ktimebomb.com/Tip/Lord/lord9838.htm

John Koskinen: "I am scheduled to fly to New York Friday evening, Dec. 31, 1999, and catch the first commercial flight back to Washington Saturday morning." ... Koskinen said he was taking the flights to show that there should be no widespread problems or social unrest caused by computers' internal calendars rolling over from 1999 to 2000. There will be some problems, however, even in computer systems that have extensive fixes installed, he warned. ... "No one can guarantee that all the systems will work."

Maybe he can sit next to the head of the FAA. Quoted on **AP** "Head of Federal Y2K Commission Confident of Fix" December 5, 1998. Submitted by Don Bionaz.
http://www.y2ktoday.com/modules/home/default.asp?id=569

John Koskinen: "We have been assured that any actions taken are not all computerised. Every action - launching a missile, engaging in any military actions - requires human intervention, so that we are reasonably confident there will not be accidents in terms of systems automatically going off on their own".

Is it just us, or is anyone else bothered by the use of the phrase "reasonably confident" in the same sentence as "launching a missile?" Quoted on **AFR Net Services** "Clinton's tsar clears Games on Y2K hurdle" October 28, 1998.
http://www.afr.com.au/content/981028/inform/inform2.html

Chapter Five:

Stupid Politicians

Elected officials have been reluctant to face up to the Y2k problem. This is due to several factors. To begin with, it requires spending money on something other than a pet project (always a difficult concept for them to grasp). It isn't a platform they can run on ("elect me and I'll spend lots of your money to ensure things stay the same"). And, since computers don't vote, they tend to ignore them...

Richmond, CA City Councilman **Nat Bates**, commenting on a preliminary audit that finds fault with the city's failure to adopt an aggressive plan to survive the millennium bug: "As long as we're moving forward then we have to just be patient and hope that eventually ... we'll achieve the level of compliance that they expect from us."

Sometime in 2002, no doubt. Quoted on **The Contra Costa Times** "Auditors bug Richmond over computer plans" December 8, 1998. Submitted by puttfxr.
http://www.hotcoco.com/news/eastbay/west/stories/kjn08804.htm

Margaret Beckett, leader of the UK House of Commons, in her latest quarterly statement to parliament on the preparations for the millennium bug: "Also, all the systems people might be worried about are designed to be "fail-safe," in other words they would cease to work rather than go off unexpectedly."

A good thing if it's a nuclear weapon: a bad thing if it's a power plant or a telephone company. Quoted on **Reuters** "UK Government Sees Good Progress on Millennium Bug" December 2, 1998. Submitted by Ree McSween.
http://www.y2ktoday.com/modules/home/default.asp?id=564&feature=&type=

An unnamed House Judiciary Committee attorney who couldn't disclose the status of the House's year 2000 disclosure bill: "We're in the midst of an impeachment proceeding."

Ah. Important work. And certainly one whose deadline is also fixed. Quoted on **Computerworld** "Inside Lines - Overheard" October 5, 1998. Submitted by Bob DeLong.

http://www.computerworld.com/home/print.nsf/all/981005liners

Senator **Phil Gramm** (R-Texas), in the weekly GOP radio address given Saturday, October 3, 1998, criticizing the Clinton administration for asking for $3.25 billion in emergency funding for federal government Y2k repairs. Noting that the current calendar was adopted in 525 A.D., he said: "The world has known that the year 2000 was coming for some 1,473 years. It is only a surprise to your administration."

Perhaps Sen. Gramm would be similarly surprised to learn that the Gregorian calendar was actually put into effect almost 416 years ago to the day on October 4, 1582, but wasn't adopted in colonial America until September 2, 1752. We wonder if it will be a surprise to *anyone* if the Federal government doesn't get all it's systems fixed in time... Quoted on **WashingtonPost.com** "Gramm Attacks Clinton Over Spending" October 3, 1998. Submitted by Steve Casburn.

http://search.washingtonpost.com/wp-srv/WAPO/19981003/V000833-100398-idx.html

Senator **Bob Bennett** (R-Utah), on his plan to set up an "early warning" system for Y2k problems by monitoring Pacific and Asian infrastructures as they roll over to 1/1/2000: "It is absolutely foolish not to use this advance notice for the good of the nation."

Now, Sen. Bennett is one of the very few politicians that understand what the Y2k problem entails, and we generally applaud his efforts to deal with it. But isn't it going to be a teensy bit late by then to do anything about it other than just watch? Quoted on **Reuters** "US Senator Looks To Pacific For Early Y2K Warning" October 5, 1998. Submitted by John Davies and David Page. By the way in case you are interested, as of this writing the rollover to 1/1/2000 will begin in the Pacific island nation of Kiribati (GMT +14) at 5am EST on December 31, 1999. New Zealand (GMT+12) will roll over at 7am EST. Zero hour for systems using GMT (UCT, Zulu...whatever) is 7pm EST, and the last few islands in the Pacific (GMT-12) roll over at 7am EST January 1, 2000. Oh, and 2000 <u>is</u> a leap year!

http://dailynews.yahoo.com/headlines/tc/story.html?s=v/nm/19981005/tc/y2k_7.html

Rep. **Dennis Kucinich**, D-Ohio: "People who know little about what the government is doing are making wild speculations."

It isn't the "wild speculations" that bother us. It's the informed speculations of Rep. Horn and Sen. Bennett that should concern people. Quoted on **Associated Press** "FAA Flying Through Y2K Renovations" September 29, 1998. Submitted by John Cox.

http://dailynews.yahoo.com/headlines/ap/washington/story.html?s=v/ap/19980929/pl/year_2000_4.html

Newt Gingrich, Speaker of the U.S. House of Representatives (at the time of the quote): "Year 2000 is total downside risk for Clinton and Gore ... If nothing goes wrong, they get no gain whatsoever. If [government computers] crash and burn, Mr. Information Superhighway has a real problem and will get a lot of heat."

Well, now *there's* a good reason to underfund the effort to keep the government from going toes up. Actually, there will probably be plenty of "heat" to go around. Quoted on **TechWeek** "Gingrich's take on Y2K" August 24, 1998. Submitted by Lee McLamb.

http://www.techweek.com/articles/8-24-98/gingrich.htm

Rep. **Constance A. Morella** (R-Md.), who chaired the House technology subcommittee hearing, reminded the audience at the Rayburn House Office Building that any substantial breakdown in the air traffic control system would not jeopardize public safety, since planes would be held on the ground, but "would obviously cause economic dislocation."

Washingtonspeak for "it would be bad." One assumes that the airlines would not put planes in the air if there was a substantial breakdown about to unpredictably occur. Quoted on **WashingtonPost.com** "FAA May Run Out of Time To Fix Y2K" August 7, 1998. Submitted by Laura A Archbald.
http://www.washingtonpost.com/wp-srv/WPlate/1998-08/07/066l-080798-idx.html

Vice President and all-round technology guy **Al Gore**: "How could this be a problem in a country where we have Intel and Microsoft?"

Asked and answered. No URL on this one, but quoted in the January 1999 issue of **Vanity Fair**, page 141. Submitted by Heather Westerfield.

Chapter Six:

Even Smart People Can Be Stupid

This always comes as such a shock. After all, you expect stupid things from stupid people. From smart people we always expect more.

We should know better by now...

Bill Gates, on the Millennium Bug issue: "There is no problem with PCs and with packaged software."

And to prove it, Microsoft has a whole section of it's web site devoted to detailing the various non-problems at www.microsoft.com/year2000. Quoted on **BusinessWorld Online** "Roundtable with Bill Gates" March 20, 1998. Submitted by Candace Skalet.

http://itmatters.bworldonline.com/bill/gates/manila/story11.html

Bill Gates again: "Any program where you still have somebody around who remembers the program, it's pretty simple to go find the place that they compare dates. You don't compare dates that many places in a program. It's in very, very few places. Even if you do it in a lot of places, there's a way of fooling the system by just taking all the dates you put in and subtracting 30 years before you put them in and adding 30 years when you put them out. There are some clever ways to get around it."

And of course, we're still awaiting Microsoft MagicBullet2000™, coming to a retailer near you real soon... Quoted on **Microsoft's** "Q&A Session with Bill Gates" May 8, 1997. Also submitted by Candace Skalet.

http://www.microsoft.com/BillGates/speeches/ceosummit/ceoQ&A.htm

Jerry Pournelle, author and pundit: "Some experts say the real problems will come from so-called embedded systems: computers installed in quite unexpected places. VCRs. Clock radios. Even my toaster and coffeemaker know what the date is. The toaster doesn't care what the year is, but one of the VCRs does, and after Jan. 1, 2000, I may not be able to program it properly: I might even miss taping an episode of "Buffy the Vampire Slayer." Once again, hardly a tragedy, although I am quite fond of Buffy. "

More small appliance concerns. And we'd feel really rained on if we couldn't tape BtVS! Quoted on **IntellectualCapital.com** "Don't Panic, Be Practical" July 30, 1998. Submitted by Paul Milne.

http://www.intellectualcapital.com/issues/98/0730/icbusiness1.asp

Jerry Pournelle, author and pundit: "But the republic has endured hurricanes, drought, the Great Freeze — remember when power plants were not working because the piles of fuel coal were frozen and had to be blasted apart with dynamite — and worse. These were events of real destruction. Property was destroyed, and people died. Computer failures are hardly in the same league."

No, they aren't. Simultaneous global computer failures are in a different league altogether. Quoted on **IntellectualCapital.com** "What to Do about the Millennium Bug" August 20, 1998. Submitted anonymously.

http://www.intellectualcapital.com/issues/98/0820/icbusiness1.asp

William Gauld, CIO, Textron Inc: "The year 2000 problem is one of the greatest things that has happened to IS. If you weren't invited before to the senior management table, you clearly are now."

Gee, you mean we could have been invited before just by screwing up something big and important? If we had only known! Quoted on **Software Magazine** "Newsfront" July 1998 Year 2000 issue. Submitted by Karen Vincent.
http://www.sentrytech.com/Y2K/Y2KJul98/y2k078nf.htm

Tom Clancy, author and would-be NFL team owner, when asked if he was concerned about the Y2k problem: "Actually, I think somebody just made that up, and if the Y2K problem, you know, the Year 2000 computer problem is real, nobody's proven it to me yet. ... Yeah, the worse thing happens is we shut down all the computers. You know, we can still live without computers. I can remember living in a world that had no computers at all."

We remember "Red Storm Rising" too, but that doesn't mean we want to read it again. Who would have guessed that the father of the techno-novel was a Luddite at heart. Quoted on **CNN.com** "Tom Clancy brings back his master of secret ops." Submitted by Adam Solomon.
http://cnn.com/books/dialogue/9808/tom.clancy.cnn/index.html

Gordon Moore, co-founder of Intel, speaking in Vienna on Intel's Y2k preparedness : "We don't know which of our production machines are going to work."

Ok, everyone say it with me: "assessment." Perhaps there should be a new "Moore's Law" regarding business systems planning. Quoted on **Reuters** "Intel's Moore Relaxed About Millennium" September 1, 1998. Submitted by Michael Taylor.

http://my.excite.com/news/r/980901/10/tech-2000

Chapter Seven:
The Unofficial Entries

When we started the Duh-2000 contest, it was our intention to only recognize stupid things said in a public forum and referenced on the web. We quickly realized that there were lots of other dumb things being said that never made it to the web, so we started an "unofficial" category. These are the things our readers have heard in meetings, heard from relatives and friends, and read in company memos. And, lest you wonder why some of these people are so dumb, remember where most of them are getting their news about Y2k...

"I'm not worried—I don't have a computer."

The ultimate extension to the "I'm not worried—I only have a PC" and the "I'm not worried—I have a Mac" attitudes. An unidentified friend of Elaine K. Kyle.

Heard on a Dutch television interview

An unnamed government official attempting to explain the Y2K problem to the general public: "Let's say someone was born in 1970. Now is the year 1999. That means this person is 1999-1970=29 years old. Now let us look forward to the year 2000. Then this person would be ... (a little pause) -30 (that is minus 30!) years old."

Quick, get out the calculator. Submitted by Karst Koymans.

My grandmother called me one night at about midnight. She told me she had the solution to the Y2K problem. She told me she couldn't talk about it on the telephone in case someone was running a wiretap. When I had a "meeting" with her several days later she made me promise that she would have a share in the profits. She then explained to me how she wanted people to use capital O's in their dates instead of zeros. This, she believed, would rectify the entire situation. If anybody decides to implement this solution on a large scale, they'd better talk to my grandmother first or else she'll be after the money!

The sad part is that some enterprising young patent attorney has probably already contacted her. Submitted by John Laur.

Overheard at a bank
Customer to Teller: Are you Y2k compliant?
Teller to Customer: I'm perfectly happy with my present long-distance carrier, thank you.

An unnamed reporter from CNBC, overheard December 28, 1998 during the announcement that the U.S. Social Security system was officially Y2k compliant (we're paraphrasing here): "Now that you have the solution for Y2K, will you be sharing it with others?"
Nope, they are keeping it to themselves. If we had a URL for this interview, we would cheerfully place it in the Stupid Journalism section. Submitted by Claudia Sawyer.

The commanding general of a combat support agency in the Department of Defense was being briefed on the progress (or lack there of) to deal with the Y2K problems in his organization. After hearing about the status of several systems — which would be ready, which would not, and what was being done about it — he interrupted and asked, "Well, what did we do the last time we had this problem?"
No comment required. Submitted anonymously.

My son...this is an adult mind you...said that the television networks wouldn't have spent all that money to renew the football season contracts for 1999-2000 if there really was a Y2k problem. That proves it: football season contract = no problem. Hope he's right.
Hey, if not we can all watch Super Bowl XXXIV by candlelight. Submitted anonymously by a parent with a very optimistic (not to mention cynical) son.

While addressing a group in Honolulu regarding potential Y2K problems, I asked the question, "What happens if some 60,000 state employees don't get their paychecks, (because the state payroll system or the mainframe computer on which it runs is non-compliant)"? One state employee in the crowd responded, "We'll strike!"
For better pay, we assume. Submitted by Dave Porter.

On seeing a piece on CNN about Y2k, my boss at work said "My neighbor next door is stockpiling food and water." "Really? What kind of work does he do?" I asked. My boss replied "He is a computer programmer." Then he asks me if our systems are Y2k compliant, to which I replied "Better start stockpiling!!!!!!"
You know you are in trouble when... Submitted by Dan Buchholz.

I was doing some consulting for a Law Firm in Milwaukee. They wanted some high speed internet access for online legal research. Their main systems were 286 based. I started talking to the head attorney about Y2K and updating his whole system, giving him Windows, etc. His response: "We are not doing anything. When the system crashes in Jan. 2000 we will sue the computer industry."

Would all of our readers who are surprised by this please raise your hands? Hmm...that's what we thought. Bravely submitted by Walt Nadolny.

Recently I decided to approach the administrator of the little hospital (our neighbor) to ask him about their y2k preparedness efforts since being the only medical facility around for miles, some of us are a little concerned. His reply; after laughing out loud he said: "Oh, I'm not worried about all that millennium bug stuff, that's just a silly hoax, and besides, by the time the year 2000 rolls around, I won't be at the hospital any longer, I'm planning on quitting around October '99 and I'm going to open up an antique furniture store!!".

Hey, come 1/1/2000 some of those manual typewriters and quill pens might come in handy! Submitted anonymously by someone who wishes to remain in the good graces of their neighbors.

I am on a Y2K committee for our company and was trying to explain to my husband the impact of the year 2000. He just could not understand how it could be such a big issue: "There wasn't a problem in 1900."

Or the other 18 century years before that, for that matter. Submitted by Melody George.

While visiting a computer store here in Toronto, I couldn't help overhearing two eager teenagers arguing about the computer purchase their mother was about to make. One teenager was sure to know every thing there is to know about the year 2000 bug, while the other one was contradicting. Right when I was about to leave one teenager said to the other "When the year 2000 gets here, the coffee cup holder won't open anymore". The salesman found it so amusing they got some free software for making his day. And also made my day.

See. We told you to stock up on Y2k compliant coffee supplies. Submitted by Hector Tamm.

I am working on Y2K for one of Australia's leading private hospitals. Part of the process involves checking the compliance of all of our suppliers. One, a small goods supplier for one of the hospital's kitchens, returned this response : "It won't effect me, I'm a supplier"
Good news! Apparently if your company is a supplier you are off the hook. Submitted by Tony.

I own a radio station here in Florida. I went in to see one of our advertisers recently and asked, "Have you heard our daily show about Y2K?" She thought for a minute and replied, "You mean the breakfast cereal?"
Snap, crackle, pop! Submitted by A.D. Whitehurst.

Another in the long line of infamous "unnamed vendors": "we're not worried about Y2K, because all of our systems are fully redundant."
In this case, that probably means their systems will fail twice. Or be twice as expensive to fix. Submitted by Trevor Holyoak.

A lawyer for one of our clients recently asked for a copy of our Y2K compliance statement. I mailed a copy to him, but he bounced it back. He wanted all references to "the year 2000" changed to "the year 2000 A.D.".

Submitted anonymously by someone obviously too close to attorneys with too much time on their hands.

My wife was recently trying to convince her sister that there was something to be concerned about regarding Y2K. The sister's response? "Well, it may be a problem for you in Texas, but we're so close to Silicon Valley (as in Santa Cruz area) that it will be fixed and won't bother us."

We're particularly worried about all those embedded cow-chips in the Lone Star state. Submitted by Wes Stalcup.

After spending several days preparing for a Y2K presentation that my boss had asked me to prepare as a community service, An employee asked me what I was working on. When I told him he responded "Oh Y2K, I know all about that. A friend of mine's father solved that problem."

Whew! That's certainly a relief. Submitted by Loren Cassell.

Response letter received upon request for Y2k compliance from an unnamed vendor:

"RE: YEAR 2000 COMPLIANCE

I refer to your recent questionnaire in relation to Year 2000 Compliance and wish to advise that these issues do not affect our Company. We currently operate a manual procedure for all systems and processes. All customers and their associated products are manually recorded.

Our Company uses PC's which are of course, not affected by the millennium bug.

It is our intention however, to move to a computer based system at some stage after the Year 2000 in order to avoid this compliance issue.

Best of luck with your Year 2000 Compliance issues."

You'll probably need it if you have a lot of vendors like this one. Submitted by Jennifer Plant.

Overheard during a Texas Highway Department planning meeting,

"Why can't we just do the same thing they did last time?"

Sometimes no comment is necessary. Submitted by Robert A. Cook.

I was sitting in a theatre before the show began and overheard two middle-aged women talking behind me. One said to the other: "If the government doesn't fix this Y2K problem— when the year 2000 comes all of the U.S. nuclear warheads are going to explode!" The other woman replied: "I hope they fix the problem fast!"
Us too. Submitted by Matt Robb.

Overheard in an elevator:
"What's the big deal? It's only computers!"
Right up there with Bill Gates' "640K ought to be enough for anybody" statement circa 1981. Submitted by Marion Orem.

An unnamed program manager of an unnamed aircraft weapons system under development by an unnamed US Air Force. When asked whether the aircraft was Y2K compliant, he responded, "The plane flies, so the software must be good."
Let's see...it didn't crash the first time we flew it so therefore that means it'll never crash. Mark that "test" phase done! Submission by a necessarily unnamed source.

One of those infamous informed sources:"If [your data] is really important, copy the material to a floppy disk, take a short break over the weekend beginning Friday December 31, 1999, get thoroughly merry if your a drinker, and return to work on Monday, January 3, and reload the disk."

Better yet, clip the disk to your metal desk with a strong refrigerator magnet so you won't lose it! Quoted in "**The Canberra Times**", the regional newspaper for Australia's capital city on July16, 1998, but not available online and therefore regrettably unofficial. Submitted by a Y2k manager down under who wishes to remain anonymous.

Un-named vendor: "As we discussed on the phone the other day, our <snip> products have no known date sensitivities. Please feel free to integrate those products into your Y2K test plans. Should you find any problems related to Year 2000, <snip> will provide you with a remedy in the form of a patch."

Sounds like they are saying: "it's not a problem unless you find out it's a problem." Is that like calories not counting if no one sees you eat them? Submitted by Ron Beraha.

And in the "almost makes sense" category:
Submitted by Eric S. Weiss, who writes: I sent out an explanation of the Year 2000 problem to members of our church who have e-mail, and briefly described what caused the problem, i.e., on 1/1/2000, many computers or computing chips will see the "00" and think that it's the year 1900, since many don't use 4-digit year codes. One person responded to me:
"I don't see why there's a problem with computers thinking it's the year 1900. Computers weren't even invented in 1900."

Management e-mail in response to a query regarding Y2k status:
"Some time ago you forwarded an inquiry from a contractor about our year 2000 plans. I would suggest the following reply. '<company name omitted> is celebrating its 100th anniversary this year. We encountered no difficulties with the year 1900 and anticipate none with the year 2000. Be assured that the company is 2000 complacent in all respects.'"
A Freudian slip if there ever was one. Submitted anonymously, but quite worthy of inclusion on the unofficial list.

The following replies were received from overseas telecommunications service providers in response to queries regarding their level of preparedness for dealing with the Y2K anomaly/"Millenium Bug":

- "I've heard about it and that is the last comment I wish to make on the subject."
- "We're not concerned because we use the Buddhist calendar and we are already in the year 2054."
- "Y2K, we're not familiar with that. However in regard to the "Millennium Bug" —not to worry my friend, we are prepared to spray everywhere."

Submitted by Ron Johnston.

"The current release is year 2000 compliant, and the next release will be even more year 2000 compliant".

Anonymous vendor response to a Y2k compliance query. Submitted by Kay Rozeboom

An unnamed manager: "I don't want anymore Y2K items on the agenda unless you can give me target dates and deliverables."

Submitted anonymously.

An unnamed armed forces deputy chief of staff: "If we don't fix the Year 2000 problem, we're just not going to make it. It's taking an incredibly long time to get that across to some of our IT community and to industry. But all I can do is persist, persist and persist. I can educate them. I can advertise our successes. Then, if they don't get it, we'll just have to shoot them."
Submitted anonymously.

I (my employer) recently purchased a RJ45 to DB25 cable from Lucent Technologies that was accompanied by a certificate affirming that "This Product is YEAR 2000 Compliant".
Cool! Can we get a Y2k compliant coffee cup to go with that? Submitted anonymously.

Chapter Eight:

Letters, Oh We Get Letters

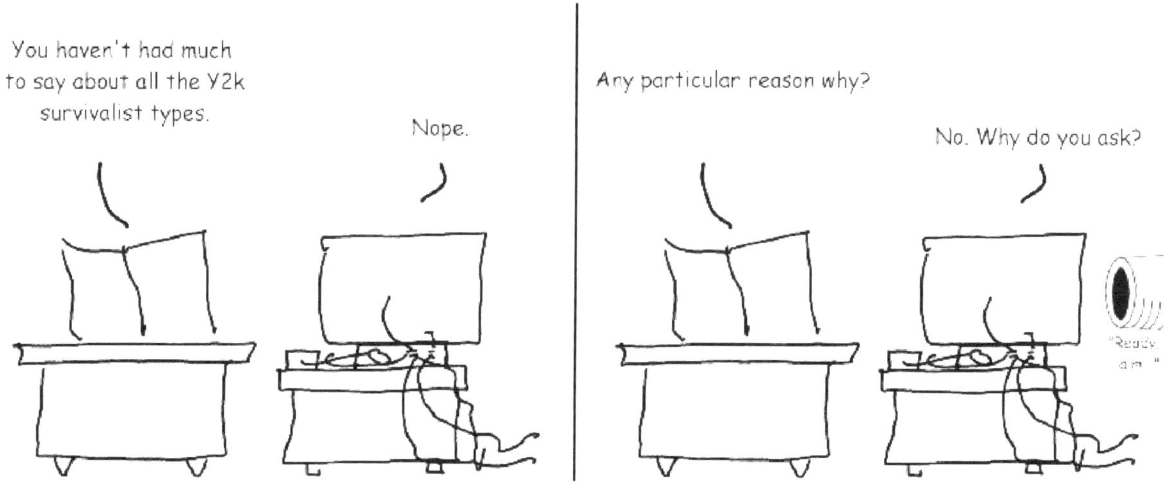

In addition to the many e-mails we get each month about stupid quotes, we get a fair amount that can only be classified as "strange." We thought you might enjoy seeing a sampling of some of the weirder ones people have sent us. Misspellings and grammatical mistakes included...

Received August 5, 1998:

The dumbest thing I've seen so far are your idiotic, self serving and stupid comments.

It's pretty obvious what you ass holes are selling. Are you guys lawyers too or just regular blood suckers?

Why don't you low lifes get real jobs instead of feeding on peoples fears.

Hey now! We're consultants not lawyers. That's at least a rung or two up the "slime" ladder. We knew we had arrived when we received our first flame.

Received August 10, 1998:

Hi! Is there a website posted where we can see all of these stupid quotes?

Er, yes there is. The one mentioned in our contest@duh-2000.com email address. And how did you send us e-mail unless you visited the page the e-mail address was published on?

Received August 23, 1998:

Bill Gates will create a new software whit the capability to be compatible whit any type of computer and to connect to any place in the internet in seconds, that everybody will buy, and in the right time he'll connect to this software taking control of every computer in the world, allowing him TO TAKE OVER THE WORLD.

If you say so. We hope it's less buggy than Win95/Win98. Just because you're paranoid doesn't mean they *aren't* out to get you.

Received August 25, 1998:

So, if I microwave popcorn on new years eve, and step out for a cold one, will the kernals continually be cremated for 1,000 years straight?

Appears to us that you've already stepped out for a cold one or two.

Received September 18, 1998:

"Yadda 2K, Yadda 2K, Yadda 2K"

It's a shame Jerry Seinfeld doesn't have anything better to do than send us e-mails in his spare time.

Received September 21, 1998:

I hesitate to write to you, because you are obviously an intelligent person who realizes the monumental trouble ahead with Y2K, and after you finish this letter (and related link), chances are you will dismiss me as a paranoid schizo who sees black helicopters behind every tree; but I assure you, I'm just an ordinary guy who thinks that Y2K will provide the opportunity that "the men behind the curtain" have been waiting for; to declare martial law, suspend the Constitution, and generally write finis to the troubling remains of democracy that keep getting in the way of international commerce and profit-taking.

This letter was prompted by the recent postin on duh-2000 of a quote about FEMA. Believe me, the LAST thing we want is for FEMA to be geared up for Y2K. Check out http://www.sonic.net/sentinel/gvcon6.html

You can check it out too. Color us skeptical. After all, the idea that a federal agency can actually carry out a coordinated effort like that is far-fetched?

Received October 17, 1998:

What if I should die before 2000, will my computer still roll over into the new milinium?

Apparently your spell checker has already given up the ghost.

Received October 29, 1998:

What if they all have minds of there own grow arms and legs and then they find chainsaws and then they start cutting peoples heads off, but our bodies are still alive and are still roaming the earth petetically forever and ever!

Nahh that will never happen

Huh? Honestly, don't you people have better things to do with your time after drinking a keg while watching Buffy the Vampire Slayer?

Received November 18, 1998:

Here is a y2k question for you. When the year 2000 comes rolling around, since all the computers will think I am 117, does that mean I get the Senior Citizen Discount at the movies?

Hey, I had a driver's license back in high school that said I was 117, but I didn't use it to get into movies...

Received November 28, 1998:

> Solution: On January 31, 1999 simply program all computers to countdown, i.e., 1999, 1998, 1997, ...
>
> That's all. That's it!

OK if you say so. And why is that any easier than programming them all to count *up* to 2000?

Received January 12, 1998:

> u r all going 2 b real disapointed when y 2000 gets here b\c the truth is MOST computers don't give a flip what the year is (mine doen't) the 1's that need 2 will even if they dont i can live a few days w/o them

Some people spend **way** too much time in chat rooms. I'd like to buy a vowel, Pat...

Received January 18, 1999:

what the heck does the k stand for??
does it meen we will resort to organisers thar are 2 kilobites??
or does it stand for KLINK GOES THE CLOCK??
or does it stand for Krap?
mabey Krud.
could be Komputer.
he he he...

or does the whole thing mean

W
H
Y 2 K
0 I
0 L
0 L
B
Y
T
E
S

WAIT THAT would be 2 megabytes!
mabey they'll have organisers that are 2 mb!

P.S <——what does that stand for?? is it y2k compliant?

Fan mail from some flounder.

Chapter Nine:

Signs Of Intelligent Life

Just when you think the planet is doomed to drown in stupidity, you find a ray of hope. If we had a few more people like these, we'd be a lot more confident that 1/1/2000 would be just another bad hangover...

Stupid Y2k Compliance Requests: One CFO's revenge

"Dan Lee, a soft-spoken former Wall Street analyst and weekend pilot, isn't generally given to flights of fancy.

But he's had it with the so-called millennium bug.

Last month, Mr. Lee, the chief financial officer of Mirage Resorts Inc. in Las Vegas, got a two-page query from Harrah's Entertainment Inc., in Memphis, Tenn., asking whether Mirage's computers are ready for the new millennium. "Who is leading your Y2K efforts?" Harrah's asked Mr. Lee, requesting titles, names and phone numbers.

Such letters are common now as companies rush to ensure that their computers will be able to cope when the date rolls from 1999 to 2000. Hoping to avoid breakdowns and legal liability for year 2000 problems, they are seeking blanket assurances from people they do business with that they, too, are millennium-prepared.

Mr. Lee scrawled in reply, "There are large rodents on the property who are in charge of our ... Y2K efforts. I'm not sure of their phone and fax numbers."

Asked for the names of his suppliers, he listed "God" and gave "Heaven" as the address. Then, in the margins, he scribbled further remarks to Colin Reed, Harrah's chief financial officer: "This is the best proof I've seen yet that the Y2K situation is a ... scheme initiated by Bill Gates, et al., to sell software."

The questionnaire he mocked specifically pertained to the computer readiness of an Atlantic City parking lot that Harrah's rents from Mirage Resorts. The lot is very low-tech. "I'm not even sure that it's paved," says the 42-year-old Mr. Lee.

So, asked by Harrah's to describe how he has tested the parking lot's systems, he responded: "We took an old Ford pickup truck and removed the clock. We then drove the Ford to the site and parked it, being careful to avoid the rodents mentioned above. It drove fine. It parked fine. We are seeking an expensive consultant who will verify, based on this data, that our parking lot is Y2K compliant."
Kudos to Dan Lee for an appropriate response to a stupid request. Quoted from **DeseretNews.com** Millennium bugged: The big Y2K problem is the silly questions December 9, 1998.

"China, as an ultimate incentive to solve the millennium bug computer problem, has ordered its airline executives to take a flight on January 1, 2000, the Financial Times said on Friday.

'All the heads of the airlines have got to be in the air on January 1, 2000,' the FT quoted Zhao Bo, in charge of dealing with the problem at the Chinese ministry of information industries, as saying.

The ministry directive coincides with a push by Beijing to minimise the risk of chaos if computer systems and electronics fail to recognize the date change from December 31, 1999 to January 1, 2000.

We really like that idea. And, it might even work. Wonder if we can get the CEO's and CFO's for the major multinationals to actually be using their own products while the clock rolls over. Quoted on **Reuters** "China Orders Airline Bosses To Fly Next Jan. 1" January 19, 1998. Submitted by Tom Lion.
http://dailynews.yahoo.com/headlines/tc/story.html?s=v/nm/19990119/tc/china_5.html